CRAM.__

Creative Games to Help Children
Learn to Think and Problem Solve
(in only 5 minutes a day!)

Ashley McCabe Mowat

Brilliant
PUBLICATIONS

We hope you and your pupils enjoy using the ideas in this book. Listed below are a few of our other books which might be of interest to you. Information on these and all our other books can be found on our website: www.brilliantpublications.co.uk.

Brilliant Activities for Gifted and Talented Children
Brilliant Activities for Stretching Gifted and Talented Children
Brain Trainers: Smart Workouts for Creative Kids (Challenges for the Rest of Us!)
Thinking Strategies for the Successful Classroom, 5–7 Year Olds
Thinking Strategies for the Successful Classroom, 7–9 Year Olds
Thinking Strategies for the Successful Classroom, 9–11 Year Olds

Published by Brilliant Publications
Unit 10
Sparrow Hall Farm
Edlesborough
Dunstable
Bedfordshire
LU6 2ES, UK

www.brilliantpublications.co.uk

The name Brilliant Publications and the logo are registered trademarks.

Written by Ashley McCabe Mowat
Illustrated by Mary McKinley
Designed by Hart McLeod

© Text Ashley McCabe Mowat 2013
© Design Brilliant Publications 2013
Printed ISBN 978-0-85747-633-3
e-book ISBN 978-1-78317-023-4

First printed and published in the UK in 2013

contents

introduction

Creative thinking is a necessary tool for survival and success. A person who can problem solve in a creative way has the potential to become a successful asset in this world. Any teacher or parent, who would like practical and user-friendly activities to help children think creatively, will love this book of trigger questions! There is so much to learn, and so little time. With this book, I have provided a fun way to learn how to think creatively and solve problems with activities that require no preparation and very little time, through exciting creative games that I call Crames.

When I teach, I see kids whose creativity is blocked. The first time I give a class a Crame, most of them stare at me dumbfounded. For example, if I said 'How many things can you think of that a pen and a finger have in common?' at first I might get a few responses such as: 'They are shaped the same' or 'they are both about the same size.' Not the most creative answers, but after practising Crames for a very short length of time I have seen dramatic improvement. Instead of only two or three responses, I will get more than 50! The quality of answers improves and they become more creative, with responses like: 'They can both be used to write' or 'they both have liquid inside them.'

The other problem is that children are afraid to make any mistakes. By allowing *every* answer to be a correct one, you will encourage them to be fluid and more creative in their ideas. Therefore, as the parent or teacher, you must always give positive feedback to ALL of the responses.

I often tell my pupils this story about a group of bankers:

> *A long time ago some bankers were having a think tank. Their problem was that people hated having to stand in long queues to get money out of the bank. They wanted to solve this and please their customers.*

> *One of the bankers raised his hand with his 'silly answer' intended to make everyone laugh and said 'Why don't we just let the customers get money out of the wall?'*

Then I pause and let the meaning sink in.

Telling this story will enable the child to understand that just because you think the idea is too 'outside the box' or too strange does not mean that it is a bad one! Did everyone 50 years ago think the technology we take for granted today was even possible? Of course they didn't! We can't be quick to judge the unconditioned minds of our children.

One reason we are not more creative is our unwillingness to break the rules we set for ourselves and our tendency to do things the same way all of the time. With these Crames, I am providing you with the tools and opportunites to look at things in different ways. Playing Crames will add variety to your day and help you and your child/pupils break out of your usual mind-set and lead you down the path of looking at the world through creative-coloured glasses!

This book focuses on many aspects of creative thinking, all of which can be exercised by playing the Crames.

- fluency
- flexibility
- originality
- elaboration
- lateral thinking

- synectics
- imagination
- problem solving
- evaluation

The Crames are broken down into categories to ensure a variety of these aspects are explored. Here are the different kinds of Crames you will find in this book:

what if...?

imagine...
envisage...
picture this...

For this Crame, you will be presented with a hypothetical situation and then the children can speculate what various outcomes might be. The focus is on fluency, flexibility, originality, imagination and risk-taking. By allowing children to express ideas without judgement, they will become more confident creative thinkers.

give me five

how can you make these 5 words into a sentence?

Once you get used to playing this one, you can ask your child or pupils to provide the words. I play this with my pupils and let them each choose one word to provide diversity. You can play this Crame with fewer or more words, depending on the age and ability of the child. My own children wake up asking for this one!

flow

how many ways can you think of...?
make a long list of...
can you think of another use for...?

This Crame focuses on fluency, flexibility, imagination, risk-taking, problem solving and critical thinking skills. It is so important to let the child go anywhere with their imagination! For example, if the activity states: *'Make a long list of ways to get to school,'* and one of the (hopefully) many responses is: 'Shrink and ride on a butterfly's wing', that's fabulous! This means that the child is successfully becoming a creative thinker! I'm sure that many amazing stories could be written about some of the ideas that you get from this Crame. Surely this is how great children's book authors come up with some of their unconventional ideas!

link

how are .... and
.... alike?

This Crame focuses on a type of thinking called synectics. Synectics is the process of finding similarities between unrelated and seemingly disconnected ideas. It 'makes the strange familiar and the familiar strange' (William J J Gordon). In this way, new possibilities become apparent. You can begin to create your own when you think of two things yourself! Better yet, let your child or pupils think of them!

stance balance perception

describe .... from different points of view.

which would you rather be...?

This Crame focuses on fluency, imagination, creative problem solving and flexibility. It also helps with risk-taking because you are forced to see things from other perspectives and make ethical decisions. The child will learn to express 'outside the box' answers aloud without judgement. In my classroom I played a Crame where we looked at the word 'charge' from many different points of view such as a ticket agent, a rock-star and a teenager. My pupils had a great deal of fun doing this and then went on to write wonderful poems and songs about the topic. They were having so much fun that they didn't realize how much they were learning (**my point exactly!**) This Crame encourages the highest level of thinking whilst producing an aware and caring creative thinker.

invent and **improve**

I think this Crame manages to target every single aspect of creative thinking found in this book. Any time you invent, you are producing an original idea. In thinking of ways to improve an already existing product or idea, you are also an inventor. Many products we use today are just improvements on existing inventions. For example: the mobile phone is just an improvement on a telephone.

Once you have used all the ideas in this book, you can keep playing this Crame by looking around you for inspiration. If I am sitting in the car with my children waiting (something mothers spend a lot of time doing), I might say... 'How many ways can you think of to improve a steering wheel?' By the end of this Crame, my steering wheel was putting on my make-up for me and providing me with a secret stash of chocolate! With practice, who knows what our future Cramers will invent?

what if?

imagine...
envisage...
picture this...

What if the sea turned every single thing it touched red forever?

What if school began at 12 midnight and lasted until 7 am?

What if it rained spaghetti instead of water?

What if there were no eggs?

What if there was no such thing as responsibility?

What if there were no bricks?

What if spiders were
as big as elephants?

imagine...
envisage...
picture this...

What if every time you sneezed, your hair grew?

What if there was no such thing as sports balls?

What if love were the only emotion you could feel?

What if everyone in the world spoke the same language?

What if there were no cows?

What if you woke up one day and all even numbers had disappeared?

What if the colour green did not exist?

What if there was no gravity?

What if green beans tasted like sweets?

imagine...
envisage...
picture this...

What if everyone in the world had blue hair?

What if people could fly?

What if there was no such thing as sugar?

What if every person had to move to a new place every three years?

What if there was no such thing as rhythm?

What if everything you touched was smooth?

What if people had four arms instead of two?

What if toys could become real if they were loved enough?

What if there was no such thing as hate?

imagine...
envisage...
picture this...

What if there was no such thing as a cycle?

What if the letter A did not exist?

What if there was no sand?

What if there was no such thing as television?

What if one pill provided all the food you needed for a day?

What if there was no plastic?

What if we could see out of our ears and hear through our eyes?

What if there was no soft, only hard?

What if mermaids were real?

What if there was no way to weigh anything?

imagine...
envisage...
picture this...

What if we could travel anywhere in the world in less than five minutes?

What if there were no trees?

What if people could only walk backwards?

What if no history had ever been recorded?

What if people were born old and became young?

What if people could only sing and not talk?

What if, instead of hands, people had tentacles?

What if there was no such thing as Monday?

What if nothing could stick?

create a sentence that makes sense with these five words...

ham, ring, elephant, rain, telephone

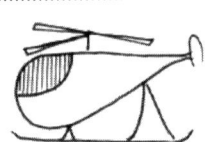

peanut, snow, globe, leg, computer

happy, perish, crab, flower, halo

library, hat, boat, tennis, forest

snow, helicopter, elegant, frog, police

clock, teeth, sock, wood, ice

weight, book, mouse, painting, key

festival, texture, news, log, clay

museum, holiday, race, magic, keyboard

insect, wheel, France, track, load

create a sentence that makes sense with these five words...

movement, wind, human, light, harvest

song, plant, stop, season, imagination

story, colour, faith, listen, roll

month, farm, gleam, row, save

float, famous, subtract, collage, home

poetry, dark, skip, balance, ship

life, batteries, clockwise, label, journey

graph, divide, general, animal, low

fact, wildlife, small, enormous, skill

pitch, island, record, pattern, horse

create a sentence that makes sense with these five words...

crawl, health, remember, glass, seaside

symmetry, question, ladybird, violin, food

nature, anger, pool, past, notebook

measure, tennis, liquid, fire, button

add, chorus, trainer, honest, sunshine

basic, double, sole, habitat, orange

join, change, Africa, science, jump

local, leotard, jockey, donate, ape

bean, jazz, hospital, doodle, quack

jellyfish, antique, lesson, swoop, frost

create a sentence that makes sense with these five words...

accelerate, bake, sketch, juggle, knock

random, wicked, promise, boomerang, ground

create, rough, symbol, familiar, cat

exaggerate, risk, straight, cup, snake

jumble, appear, soda, song, dangerous

generous, magnet, navigate, blue, argue

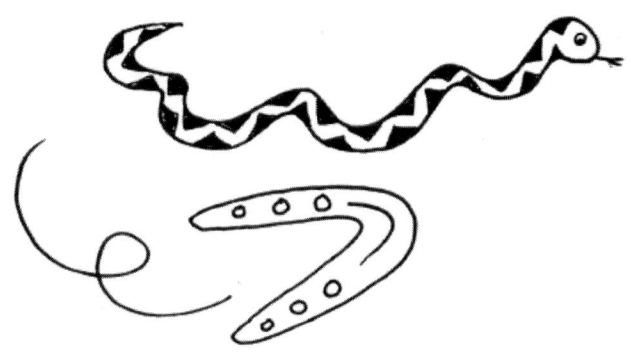

create a sentence that makes sense with these five words...

necklace, identical, cruel, face, drawer

audience, sting, pink, pasta, misbehave

cure, adapt, branch, kangaroo, march

flow

how many can you think of...

things that **sink**

things that you can't **touch**

names for a **sea monster**

books that **feature** a colour in the title

things that **pop**

things people in the future might do for **entertainment**

reasons to find two dead birds in your **garden** every single morning

things that are **invisible**

things that you can't **hear**

how many can you think of...

embarrassing things

things that make you feel **frustrated**

names for a **band** that sings children's songs

things that have **lines** on them

things you can **throw**

things that you could **do** to show someone that you **care**

exciting and **original names** for a sweet shop

things that are both **soft** and **strong**

things that **open**

things in the **sky**

how many can you think of...

ideas that come to your mind when
you hear the word **chocolate**

titles for a book about **space**

things that **light up**

things that are **attached**

themes for a children's party

things you would leave in a time capsule for people to find
in the **future**

things you can do on a **wall**, or to a wall

things that **close**

things that **squeak**

titles for a song about **food**

how many can you think of...

things that a **tongue depressor** could be used for (other than doctors looking at your throat)

things that **wax** could be used for

things that are **silly**

interesting and **original** names for a roller skating rink

things that have **pockets**

reasons why you might be late for **school**

titles for a **song** about trees

things **found** in water

reasons you need to go shopping

things that might make you say **'ouch'**

how many can you think of...

ways to make shade on the beach with no **umbrella**

ways to get in **shape** with no equipment

uses for a **towel** (other than drying something)

uses for a can opener (other than opening cans)

how many can you think of...

ways you can escape from a locked room without a key

ways to **congratulate** someone

ways to **stick** something together

ways you can say 'thank you' to someone who really **deserves** it

ways to **support** a friend who is very shy

ways to **stop** crime

ways to make new **friends**

uses for a **potato**

uses for a bag of **sand**
(other than filling a sandbox)

how many can you think of...

things you can **throw** away

things that are **yellow** or mellow

things that **use** water

things that go **together** like socks and shoes

ways that you could **injure** yourself

things you might do on a **journey**

combinations of **opposites**: thick and thin, big and small…

things that can **fly**

titles for books about **dance**

reasons to **avoid** something

things that give you a **chill**

how many can you think of...

things that make you **laugh**

things that make you **scream**

reasons why you need to **defend** someone

things that have **no colour** (black or white, or both)

You have been given the opportunity to go to Africa and help build houses for people who don't have them. However, without funds, you won't be able to go! **How many ways can you think of to raise money to participate in this exciting experience and philanthropic trip?**

link

remember the brainstorming rules – when you think there are no ideas left, try to come up with at least five more...

In what ways are a pair of flip-flops and an umbrella alike?

In what ways are stripes and zigzags the same?

In what ways are a clown and a violinist the same?

In what ways are a rocket and a biro the same?

In what ways are a plant and a pen alike?

What do 'extraordinary' and 'mouse' have in common?

In what ways are an orchard and a suitcase alike?

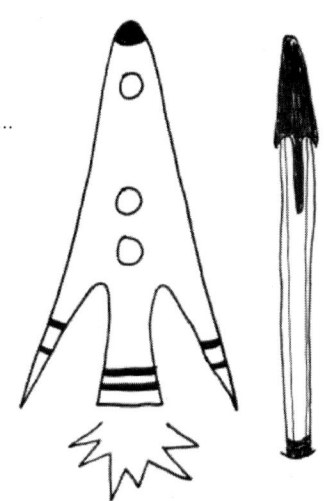

when you think there are no ideas left, try to come up with at least five more...

In what ways are the words 'limp' and 'drum' the same?

In what ways are a circuit and a planet the same?

In what ways are a teacher and the world the same?

In what ways are a book and a computer the same?

In what ways are the colours white and black the same?

In what ways are a biro and a finger the same?

In what ways are pockets and lockets the same?

In what ways are dolphins and peacocks the same?

In what ways is a puzzle like an argument?

when you think there are no ideas left, try to come up with at least five more...

In what ways are hands like songs?

In what ways is a melody like sugar?

In what ways are a box and an idea the same?

How is a door like a painting?

How is a museum like a story?

How is a hero like ketchup?

How is a dream like a sandwich?

How is a forest like a tennis ball?

when you think there are no ideas left, try to come up with at least five more...

How is an acrobat like a helicopter?

How is a rose like a ballerina?

How is homework like a garden?

How is a supermarket like a school?

How is a glowing sign like a daisy?

stance...

Describe the word **traffic** from these different points of view: a policeman, a mother, an environmentalist, a baby, a shop owner and a restaurateur.

Describe the word **snow** from these different points of view: Santa, a pilot, a headmaster/headmistress, a child and a snowboarder.

Argue the fact that you believe that it is a **good idea** to cut down trees. (Even if you don't!)

What is your **least** favourite colour? Now, choose that colour and explain why you think it is the best colour on the planet! (Even if you don't!)

Describe the word **magical** from these different points of view: a fairy, a magician, a doctor, an orphan and an astronaut.

stance...

Describe how each of the following **could feel** about Goldilocks: Mother Bear, cold porridge, Goldilocks' own mother, Goldilocks' hair and her shoes!

Describe how each of the following **could feel** about a football: a child, a nurse, a manufacturer of footballs, a field and parents.

What is your **least** favourite food? Now choose that food and pretend that you love it! Convince someone else to eat it.

Describe how a computer might **feel** about the following: a student, a cleaner, an off button, a toddler and a new model computer.

How could the word **crafty** describe the following people/things: hair, a dresser, a carpenter, a child, a blogger (or journalist) and a sales assistant?

stance...

Describe the word **disaster** from these different points of view: rainforest, ocean, dog, bee and countryside.

What is the worst thing that you can think of about homework? Give at least ten reasons why homework is **fantastic**!

Describe the word **feather** from these different points of view: a dancer, a swan, an antique dealer, a pillow and a snake.

How might a **fountain** feel about: coins, a photographer, birds, something little and algae?

How does the colour **pink** feel about: Valentine's Day, little girls and little boys?

Describe the word **tender** from these different points of view: a songwriter, a builder, a feather, a doctor and an athlete.

balance...

Would you rather be a jewel or a flower? *Why?*

Would you rather win an Olympic medal or make a great discovery? *Why?*

Would you rather be a sphere or a cube? *Why?*

Would you rather be hungry or sad? *Why?*

Would you rather be a bus or a lake? *Why?*

Would you rather be a painting or a mobile telephone? *Why?*

Would you rather be a teacher's desk or a whiteboard? *Why?*

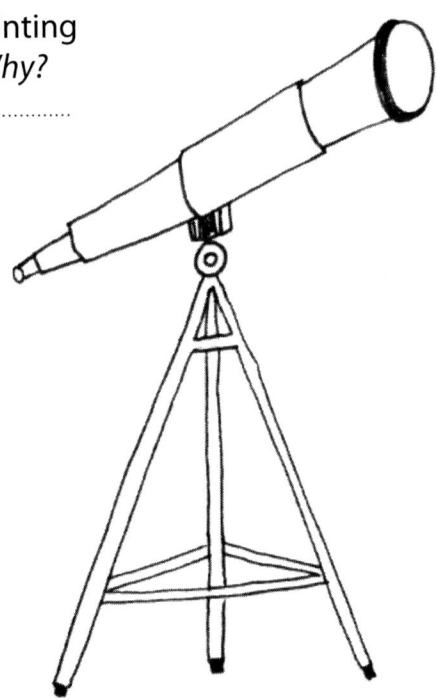

balance...

Would you rather be a telescope or a star? *Why?*

Would you rather be lucky or funny? *Why?*

Would you rather be a piece of spaghetti or an earthworm? *Why?*

Would you rather be a clock or a train? *Why?*

Would you rather be a piece of paper or a pencil? *Why?*

Would you rather be a sock or a shoe? *Why?*

Would you rather be the number 2 or the number 200? *Why?*

Would you rather be a pencil case or a bottle? *Why?*

Would you rather travel by horse or by car? *Why?*

balance...

If you could only do one but not both, would you rather be able to sing or dance? *Why?*

Would you rather be a notebook or a robin? *Why?*

Would you rather be jeans or a locket? *Why?*

Would you rather be a scarecrow or a jellyfish? *Why?*

Would you rather be marble or linen? *Why?*

Would you rather be a picture or a fish tank? *Why?*

Would you rather be a throne or a fold-away chair? *Why?*

Would you rather be a seed or a flower? *Why?*

Would you rather be an airport or an arena? *Why?*

perception...

Four traits that can really help you succeed with a task are commitment, creativity, caring and courage. Discuss why you need all of these traits combined to achieve your goals.

Finish this sentence at least 10 times: I CAN...(try to come up with answers that nobody else would think of!)

How does gentle look?

Using beautiful and creative words, describe a flower just after a rainstorm.

Choose an item that might be found in a child's packed lunch. Describe the item as if it were on a menu in one of the world's best restaurants. For example: an orange – a succulent, tropical fruit that explodes sensational juices into your mouth!

perception...

How does red feel?

Try to have a conversation with someone where you are only allowed to express yourself in terms of nature. For example: 'In my last lesson, I felt like a river was flowing from my head!'

Choose a special cause that you feel strongly about. Think of creative ways that you could raise support for this cause or inform other people about it.

How does purple smell?

Imagine that you found the following items in a box while digging in your back garden: a light bulb, a can of soda, a beach towel, a computer game and a CD player. How many ways can you think of to describe the person that buried the box?

perception...

How does desperate sound?

Give at least 5 reasons why it is important to be creative in each of these five careers: teacher, judge, editor, fireman and photographer.

Choose a problem in your home, school or community. Make a long list of possible solutions.

How does brown feel?

How does the sun taste?

Imagine that you found a box in the dark. You reach into it and feel something soft. How many things can you think of that it could be?

How does brilliant sound?

How does delicate smell?

perception...

Describe a dolphin swimming in the sea.

How does clever look?

Describe how you think a window feels about the inside and the outside.

Which is sharper, a grin or a scowl?

invent...

a new creature made up from two existing ones

a new piece of playground equipment. What would you call it?

a new way to paint a room

a new way to tie your shoes

a new device to help you drink something

something to help you get dressed quicker or more easily

something using these three words: cork, telephone, boot

something that links these three words: hand, ice-cream, television

something that uses sand

something for the kitchen

invent...

something for a classroom

something that helps you eat ice-cream without making a mess

a new way to open a door

a special handshake to show friendship

a new way to listen to music

something that uses these three words: cling, explore, coast

something that uses these two words: glide, fragile

a new way to reuse a scrunched up piece of paper

a new way to wash a car

something that will help people to remember to switch off lights

invent...

a new way to sweep the floor

a new way to empty the dishwasher

a new way to travel to school

something that a dog would like

a new holiday that celebrates music

something that helps keep cereal from pouring out of the box and going everywhere!

Improve... how could you improve...

a surfboard

a pair of trainers

a toothbrush

a bicycle

improve...

a tennis racket

a front door

glasses

a skyscraper

your school

a walking stick

a lunch table

a hat

a shopping bag

the inside of an airport

improve...

a piano or musical instrument

a glue stick

a hula hoop

a milk container

a box

a fork

a refrigerator

a rucksack

a clock

a beach towel

a belt

a chair

improve...

a chest of drawers

a sink

a bathtub

a pair of jeans

an aeroplane

a glass jar

a coat

a pair of roller skates

a football

a seat in the cinema

a staircase

a restaurant to make it more fun for children